DALMATIANS

DALMATIANS

JULIE MARS

Photographs by Isabelle Français

Ariel Books

Andrews and McMeel

Kansas City

Design by Jaye Zimet

Photographs copyright © 1996 by Isabelle Français

ISBN: 0-8362-2112-5

Library of Congress Catalog Card Number: 96-83364

CONTENTS

INTRODUCTION

Think of the dalmatian, and visions of a bygone era come instantly to mind, an era when the cry of "Fire!" brought with it the pounding of a team of horses through crowded city streets. Who could imagine this scene without the powerful, black-and-white dalmatian tearing along ahead of the wagon wheels, inches from the hooves of the galloping horses? Or perhaps we picture an old-fashioned beer wagon loaded with barrels, a dalmatian perched proudly at the driver's side.

These images from the past may be long gone, but not the dalmatian. In fact, the strangely beautiful dalmatian is more popular than ever before. Each

time Walt Disney rereleases the animated film *One Hundred and One Dalmatians*, it spurs an increase in the number of registered dalmatians. When the film opened in Britain in 1959, registrations there doubled from seven hundred to fourteen hundred dogs per year. In the United States, the American Kennel Club (AKC) now registers over five thousand new dalmatians each year.

Many dalmatian owners insist that, given the right circumstances, their dogs will draw their lips back and break into a toothy—and very recognizable—grin. Breeders attribute the grin to a recessive genetic trait. Unfortunately, the grin seems to happen most frequently when the dalmatian is caught "red-handed" in some naughty mischief. It is usually accompanied by a head lowered in shame as the dog slinks away from the scene of the crime. Owners report that it is difficult to keep a straight face when confronted by a dalmatian with a guilty smile.

Good-natured, energetic, and charming, dalmatians have so secured their place in the hearts of dog lovers everywhere that they consistently rank among the ten most popular dog breeds.

Whether your interest is in a show dog or a household pet, the dalmatian dog, with his crazy spots and his boundless enthusiasm, is a definite, first-place winner.

YOUR DALMATIAN

HISTORY OF
THE BREED

Dalmatian lovers, determined to trace the history of the breed, often point to the frequent occurrence of spotted dogs in ancient engravings, statues, paintings, and even written accounts to make their case for the birthplace of the dalmatian breed. A spotted dog that could be a dalmatian, for example, appears in the

Tomb of Redmera on the Nile River—in a painting dated 3000 B.C.! Despite the best efforts of many canine researchers, the exact origin of the dalmatian remains a mystery.

One popular theory holds that the dalmatian's first home was the province of Dalmatia on the Adriatic Sea near the Gulf of Venice. This theory provided the

name for the breed. Others speculate that early dalmatians accompanied Romany gypsy bands on their worldwide travels, thereby accounting for the mysterious omnipresence of the dog in ancient artwork.

By the mid-1700s, however, the name "dalmatian" was used everywhere to describe the breed, and from that point forward, their history is well documented. Dalmatians have loyally served as military and sentinel dogs, draft dogs, shepherds, trail dogs, bird dogs, and retrievers. In each of these canine occupations, dalmatians have performed with agility, intelligence, and skill.

But it is their work as lead dogs for horse-drawn vehicles that has become the most famous. Legend has it that British aristocrats of the eighteenth century, enamored by the beautiful but odd appearance of dalmatians, brought them home to England from their grand tours of Europe. Soon dalmatians became a crucial part of the ostentatious horse-and-carriage processions of the idle rich. Unafraid of horses, dalmatians trotted along under the rear axle or beneath the pole between the horses. Later, many were trained to precede the horses.

From there, it was a natural progression to the duties of fire-dog. Dalmatians tore through the streets ahead of the fire wagon, clearing the path and warning onlookers that an emergency vehicle was approaching at high speed. Noted for their seemingly limitless endurance for running, the breed was per-

fectly suited to these duties. Back at the firehouse, dalmatians earned their keep by eliminating the rats and other rodents. Even today, the dalmatian remains a popular firehouse mascot, and the sight of a spotted dog riding a speeding, red fire truck adds to the thrill and drama of a rescue-in-progress.

Another arena where the dalmatian found a natural home was the circus. Energetic, amusing, highly trainable, and charming in their appearance, dalmatians soon became a fixture in traveling carnivals and stage shows all across Europe. They delighted audiences by

leaping through hoops, leading clowns on merry chases, and performing daredevil tricks such as charging between the legs of horses in the ring. Along the way, dalmatians acquired many nicknames, such as the Plum-Pudding Dog, Firehouse Dog, English Coach Dog, Dally, Coach Dog, the Bengal Harrier, and Spotted Dick.

As a breed, the dalmatian's popularity received a great boost in 1959 from the Walt Disney film *One Hundred and One Dalmatians*. This beloved children's classic, rereleased periodically for many decades, created wave after wave of Dal-mania, and the number of American Kennel Club registered dalmatians rose steadily until the dalmatian entered the elite group of the ten most popular breeds—where it remains.

A reliable worker, an energetic

companion, a beautiful dog, and a great family pet, the dalmatian's future looks as fascinating and bright as its interesting and unusual past.

PHYSICAL CHARACTERISTICS

The "breed standard" is the official description of an ideal purebred dog. It is carefully written by the members of the national dog club for the purpose of maintaining the purity and health of the breed. Once the breed standard is approved (in the U.S.A., by the American Kennel Club), each dog-show judge implements it by measuring the actual contestant dog against this abstract standard of complete canine excellence. There may, however, be slight differences in standards for the same breed from country to country.

A dalmatian is essentially a black or liver-colored dog that carries a special gene for "white masking." This means that the white color covers most of the background coat, leaving dark spots that appear in a variety of shapes, from splotches and patches to perfectly round dots.

A great deal of attention is paid to the dalmatian's spots. Their color should be dense black or liver brown, and their shape should be round and well-defined, ranging in diameter from dime- to quarter-size. The spots that appear on the head, ears, legs, tail, and face should be smaller than those on the body, and no spots should intermingle, though it is permissible that they touch. In formal competition, your dalmatian would face disqualification for patches (a solid, sharply defined mass of color that is larger than the other markings on the dog), a mix of three colors in the coat, or markings in any color other than black or liver.

An ideal dalmatian is a strong, alert, and active dog capable of great endurance and good speed. He should be intelligent in his expression, symmetrical in outline, and free of shyness. His ears should be set high and close to the head. He should have a deep chest,

a powerful back, and a gradually tapering tail that's strong at the base and carried with a slight upward curve.

Your dalmatian should stand between 19 and 23 inches high at the shoulders, and weigh about 50–55 pounds. His head should be moderately long; his eyes should be of medium size, round, bright, set well apart, and rimmed in black (for black and white dalmatians) or brown (for liver and white dalmatians). A height of over 24 inches is unacceptable for conformation competition, as are flesh-colored eye rims.

BEHAVIORAL
CHARACTERISTICS

A dalmatian is a naturally curious dog that learns quickly and possesses seemingly endless energy. This winning combination leads to a great deal of fun and amusement—but it also guarantees that your dalmatian will get into his share (or perhaps a bit *more* than his share) of mischief.

A dalmatian will instinctively test his owner's interpretation of "the boundaries," so a wise owner will make sure he or she comes out best every time! If you let your dog win once, you may face a very serious challenge in reasserting yourself as the alpha member of the pack. Your dalmatian will follow the rules if you repeatedly communicate them in a clear, consistent manner. Be patient! Part of your dog's charm is his wily determi-

nation to have his own way, if at all possible.

Dalmatians are notoriously people-oriented and love to be with their owners. They are very affectionate— once *they* decide that you have passed the test. A look at their history reminds us that dalmatians have always been actively involved in work that requires good judgment and precision—like avoiding the horse's pounding hooves! Remembering that, we can well understand that they are independent and like to be left alone to assess a newcomer.

The breed standard calls for a

stable and dignified temperament, and most dalmatians will demonstrate this in any new situation. But once the relationship between dog and owner has been struck, the dalmatian becomes an exuberant, playful greeter and a willing, fun-loving companion. Without any training, dalmatians exhibit caring protectiveness of their owner and family. In return, they crave—and demand—your undivided attention and love.

Your dalmatian, bred over hundreds of years for endurance and speed, requires regular exercise. However, a dalmatian won't stop until you do, so be

sure not to overtax a puppy or older dog. He needs exercise, but never to the point of complete exhaustion.

Reputable dalmatian breeders take enormous pride in the overall good temperament of the dalmatian. Rumors that dalmatians tend to be nervous, high-strung, or hyper are just that—rumors. Given the care and attention that he needs, a dalmatian makes a perfect show dog and a loving household pet.

YOUR DALMATIAN PUPPY

CHOOSING A PUPPY

Once you have decided that a dalmatian is the right dog for you, you can begin the joyous pursuit of the right puppy. You should approach this pleasant task quite seriously because your goal is to find the specific dog that you will best relate to, physically, psychologically, and emotionally.

If possible, you should view the litter when the puppies are three to four weeks old. If you select your pup then, you can be well acquainted by the time the puppies are ready to leave their mother—usually around eight weeks.

Bear in mind, though, that many breeders do not permit potential buyers to see or touch the puppies (and they may not set a price) until the pups are seven weeks old, when their qualitative distinctions are somewhat clear.

All dalmatian puppies are born pure white. Over the first few weeks of life, their spots will appear as dull smudges and then change to bold dots. In choosing your dalmatian pup, experts suggest that you avoid a defensive puppy who seems frightened by humans or other dogs. They advise potential buyers to study the litter carefully, however, because there's a clear difference in temperament between a shy pup and a frightened one. Shy puppies often make excellent pets and show dogs. Many shy pups blossom when they leave the pecking order of the litter, but a defensive puppy might grow up with behavioral problems.

A professional trainer or breeder should supply a formal purchase agreement for a purebred dalmatian puppy. The agreement will include the dog's sex, birth date, color, purchase price, and AKC registration numbers for his parents. (You should also receive an AKC application so you can register your puppy.)

Some purchase agreements include conditions to the sale of the puppy or even its future use. The agreement may not allow any breeding of the dog at all, or the seller may maintain all

or some of the future rights to breeding the dog. The buyer may be required to agree to use the dog *only* for the intended purpose given in the agreement; in competition, for instance. Some breeders will also supply a written guarantee that the puppy will not exhibit common genetic diseases.

PUPPY CARE

Your dalmatian puppy relies on you to keep him healthy. Initially, this important responsibility includes feeding your puppy properly, socializing him within his new environment (see "Bonding"), and seeing that he receives all the necessary shots at the right time. All puppies need to be vaccinated with a series of shots, beginning sometime between the eighth and twelfth week of age. Even though the first visits to the vet are often traumatic, your puppy needs these vaccinations, which protect him from distemper, hepatitis, coronavirus, leptospirosis, and parvovirus. A series of vaccinations for rabies will also be necessary.

Additionally, your vet will check your puppy's stool for signs of worms—

some of them deadly. Most puppies have some type of worms, so don't be surprised if yours does too. They can be quickly and effectively eliminated with the right kind of medication from your vet.

Your pup will be weaned by the time he comes home with you. Since the first few days in his new home are a very stressful time for the puppy, obtaining a supply of the same food he is already used to is one way of reducing the number of changes the puppy has to make. Feeding him smaller portions for a while may also reduce stomach upsets. You should avoid giving the puppy milk unless he has been used to milk in his diet, and avoid giving him milk during the last feeding at night to help reduce the chance of diarrhea.

Your puppy should have three meals a day at regular times—morning,

noon, and early evening. Remember, he burns up more energy—and more calories—than an adult dog. Give your young pup water at frequent intervals, but remove the water dish at night during the house-training period.

At about six months you can

begin to give your puppy two meals a day. Each meal should last fifteen to twenty-five minutes. The size of portions should be monitored carefully; if your puppy is not eating all his food, try giving him less next time; do not let uneaten food sit out.

The best commercial kind of puppy food is the all-in-one dry food called kibble. Experts recommend that this comprise 100 percent of your dalmatian puppy's diet. Soaking the kibble in warm water for ten to fifteen minutes before feeding helps prevent bloat. If the puppy is healthy, supplements to commercial foods are unnecessary and may even be dangerous to the long-term health of your dog.

BONDING

Leaving his mother and his littermates may transform your playful puppy into a frightened, vulnerable little animal. Your pup needs special treatment as he experiences the biggest adjustment of his short life. Experts suggest that you remain with your puppy twenty-four hours a day, if possible, during the critical bonding period from eight to twelve weeks. This is the time when your puppy will form a permanent bond to his "pack"—you and your family. Owners frequently settle the puppy in a wire crate at night right next to the owner's bed

so the puppy can relax in the feeling of closeness and security even while he sleeps.

This short period of extra attention will

form the foundation of a very deep and necessary bond between puppy and owner. Without it, your puppy may grow up feeling insecure and isolated. Eye contact, repetition of your puppy's name, talking to him in a soft, comforting voice, praising, and petting are all critical parts of the bonding experience—dog owners agree that the bond ties them to the puppy just as tightly as it ties the puppy to the owner.

BASIC TRAINING

Training your dog requires patience, consistency, and, possibly most necessary, a sense of humor. It is particularly important to remember that your puppy is a baby. Some of his "mistakes"—particularly urinating or soiling inside—may be a developmental, not a disciplinary, issue. He's just too young to "hold it." Never punish a dog for what he is incapable of correcting because of his age. Rather, train yourself to recognize and meet your puppy's needs.

There are three basic lessons a

dalmatian—or any dog—should learn, and your puppy will learn them quickly if you approach the training in the right way. The first lesson is housebreaking. To teach your puppy to "go" outside requires that you take him out frequently, particularly when he exhibits behaviors such as pacing, sniffing the ground, or squatting. A firm "No" will stop the dog from urinating; then carry him out to an area that's been designated for his elimination. Praise him highly when he does what you want.

Likewise, treat "slips" in a very specific manner. Bring your pup to the

scene of the accident and sternly scold him. It is never necessary to humiliate your dog, as some owners do, by pushing his face into the feces. He will learn better by praise and encouragement. To get your puppy through the night, prepare *yourself* to take him out when he whines or restlessly paces. Remember, he may be more than three months old before he can make it through the entire night without urinating.

Secondly, your puppy should learn his name. Repeat it frequently. A good exercise is to walk around your yard for about ten minutes a day, saying his name and encouraging him to follow you. (Your puppy will naturally do this.) This reinforces his name and also teaches him to come when called—a very important lesson.

Finally, teach your puppy that

"No" means "Stop what you are doing right now." Your pup will get the message quickly if you simply raise your voice. Stop all destructive behavior (such as nipping, chewing, and mouthing) firmly and quickly. It will save you much aggravation later.

More formal obedience training can begin when the puppy is about six months old. The goal is to teach your dog to follow verbal commands without being corrected by a leash and collar. You can encourage the puppy by rewarding him with an activity he enjoys right after a training session. Enrolling the puppy in a puppy socializing class may be particularly helpful in preparing him for a training class later. Socializing the puppy by taking him outside and accustoming him to other people, animals, and such moving objects as cars and bicycles is also important.

Your Adult Dalmatian

FOOD

In order for your dog to remain in optimum health, he needs the complete daily nourishment provided by a carefully balanced diet. The amount your dog consumes will depend on his weight and his activity level. Young adult dalmatians, for example, generally eat six to nine cups of dry kibble per day. A middle-aged dog—six to eight years old—may gain weight on that amount, and his diet should be adjusted accordingly. Your dalmatian should be lean but not skinny for his whole life.

Dalmatians have an unusual and unique metabolism that requires careful monitoring, and it is extremely important that their owners familiarize themselves with the dietary restrictions this condition imposes. Unlike other dogs, dalmatians do not properly metabolize purines (chemical compounds found in certain meat and vegetable products). Most dogs convert purines during digestion to uric acid and then convert the uric acid to a substance called allantoin for excretion. Dalmatians are unable to complete this final transformation of uric acid to allantoin, and consequently they are in a high-risk group for kidney and bladder stones.

To avoid these potentially life-threatening problems, adult dalmatians should eat a diet containing not more than 20 percent protein. You should *never* feed your dalmatian organ meat or wild game. Avoid canned or dry food that lists red meat or poultry as one of the first three ingredients. Don't be surprised if other dog owners scoff at your fastidiousness. Of all the dog breeds acknowledged by the AKC, *only* dalmatians have these specific dietary restrictions.

Feed your adult dalmatian twice a day. Continue to soak the kibble for easier digestion. It is very important to wash your dog's feeding dishes and bowls daily. Ceramic or stainless steel bowls and dishes are more durable and easier to keep clean than plastic ones. Although you should clear away any leftover food, clean water should always be easily available for the dog.

TRAINING AND EXERCISE

Training a dalmatian begins when he is still a puppy. You can teach your dog the words for activities when he is still young, and help him learn to concentrate

in order to make training easier. Rewarding a dalmatian with praise and petting for a job well done is much more effective as a training basis than punishing him for failures. Speaking firmly, without either shouting or scolding, and then praising a dog's successes will yield the best results.

In the beginning, limit your training sessions to fifteen minutes. Make it clear to your dog when training is beginning and ending, and always play with him for a while afterward. Be patient; your dog will ultimately learn to obey specific commands if you stay with it. *Sit, heel, stay, come,* and *down* are the absolute minimum vocabulary for a well-trained dog.

Formal obedience training provided by a professional trainer aims at producing a dalmatian who will understand and obey any specific command instantly. But even without conducting formal training themselves, owners need to participate with their dogs in a variety of activities. All dogs need exercise each day in order to be content, and an energetic dog like a dalmatian needs more than most. A daily two-mile walk and perhaps a long session of ball throwing

are the absolute minimum. Be prepared to commit yourself to some serious exercise and playtime if you're considering raising a dalmatian!

GROOMING

Many owners, fooled by the clean, sleek appearance of the dalmatian's coat, are unpleasantly surprised to learn that, like all dogs, dalmatians shed. And mischievous as they can sometimes be, they get dirty too. This calls for the occasional bath. Dalmatians do best if you use a quiet, gentle spray apparatus or nozzle and a mild shampoo or soap. Take extra care around your pet's eyes. If you get soap in them, you may never be allowed to bathe your dalmatian again!

Be sure to rinse thoroughly, and

monitor your dog's skin and lips for any redness or sign of a rash. (This could indicate an allergic reaction to the soap.) Dry him well, and complete his grooming by trimming his cowlicks, whiskers, and tail. Every couple of weeks the grooming

session should include checking and cleaning your dalmatian's ears, always, of course, without probing.

Though exercise on rough ground or pavement should help keep your dalmatian's nails short, they may still need trimming from time to time. You can ask your veterinarian to show you how to clip his nails (always with a special dog clipper). Keeping his teeth clean by rubbing them with gauze or a soft tooth-brush dipped in a paste

of half baking soda, half hydrogen peroxide will help prevent serious problems. Still, any significant plaque buildup will require a visit to the vet for scaling.

HEALTH

An annual visit to the veterinarian for a physical exam is an indispensable part of caring for your pet. After his first series of shots, your dalmatian will need annual boosters, and the exam should always include a check for worms.

Like many other white-coated animals (cats, rabbits, and mice, for example), dalmatians are susceptible to hearing problems and even deafness. In fact, the Dalmatian Club of America indicates that about 8 percent of dalmatians are completely deaf, while 22 percent hear in one ear only. As a pet, a dog with hearing in one ear only is nearly indistinguishable from a dog with full hearing, but a completely deaf dalmatian presents a caretaking challenge that few owners can realistically meet. Responsible breeders test for hearing loss. They recommend euthanasia for deaf puppies, viewing this as the most humane response to a serious problem. This deaf-ness is genetic and can only be lessened through selective breeding.

Dalmatians, like all dogs, need protection from the elements when they are left outside, a shelter from exces-sive heat or cold. Dogs who venture out-side are also susceptible to fleas, ticks, and mites. Ticks can be individually removed with tweezers, but remember to protect yourself. Ticks carry diseases that humans can catch, such as Lyme disease. Probably the best way to get rid of bugs is by using a special powder or spray. In serious cases you may need to bathe your dog with an insecticidal shampoo and wash all his bedding as well.

THE SHOW CIRCUIT

Showing and judging the conformation of dogs is considered a sport: the dog sport. Each year in the United States there are over ten thousand competitive events—dog shows, field trials, obedience trials. Each of the AKC-registered breeds has a national parent club that helps sponsor and organize licensed shows of various kinds.

The dog show, which emphasizes

onformation, or how close competitors come to achieving the breed standard, is the most common kind of show. Cate-

gories for entry in a given show can include Puppy (sometimes divided into two separate age classes of six to nine months and nine to twelve months), Novice, Bred-by-Exhibitor, American-Bred, and Open. At licensed events, competitors win points toward titles. Overall winners of shows sponsored by individual breed clubs earn the title Best of Breed, and all-breed clubs sponsor shows leading to the title of Best in Show. Five points is the maximum a competitor can win in one show; a dog that has won fifteen points in AKC-licensed shows is an AKC champion.

The best known and most presti-
gious dog show in the United States is
the annual event put on by the Westminster Kennel Club in New York. Every dog
that enters Westminster is already a
champion, and some exhibitors enter the
competition simply for the honor of saying that their dogs participated in the
Westminster show; the annual show book
is a cherished keepsake.

The responsibility of a judge is
heavy, and judges themselves are subject
to strict requirements before they are
accredited by the AKC. A judge is
expected to have had at least ten years'

dog-show experience before applying to be certified, must specify which breed (or breeds) he or she wishes to evaluate, must have owned or exhibited dogs of that breed, and must have bred at least four litters of the same breed. Furthermore, a candidate must have had five AKC stewarding assignments, pass a rules test and a test on breed standards, and supply references, in order to be accredited.

It is the judges who determine the winners of a show, but a judge can only make a decision about the best dog in any category on the basis of the field of competitors at that single event and on that single day. The knowledge that on a different day, and in a different field of competitors, the judgments might well be very different, is part of the essence of the dog sport, a source of its fascination and its drama.